"Ann and Bob Redd provide sage advice for anyone over 50 faced with retirement or career transition. A fine coat of humor enhances sensible comments on work, play, and family relationships. The ultimate message is that it's never too late to live with purpose. **Whimsey, Wit and Wisdom** *is highly recommended."*
  - **Ms. Lawrence Webster**
    Public Services Librarian
    Venice, Florida

"In **Whimsey, Wit and Wisdom**, *the Redds claim that humor saved the day more than once during their transition into the golden years; easy, fun reading."*
  - **Pat Butrin-Geurink**
    Grand Rapids Press
    Grand Rapids, Michigan

"Very brightly and briskly done! Wonderful, impish humor."
  - **Dr. Donald Holmes**
    Traverse City, Michigan

*"***Whimsey, Wit and Wisdom** *is a book for everyone over 50 who enjoys good humor and lively cartoons."*
  - **Mr. James Mahoy**
    Attorney
    Mechanicsburg, Ohio

"This book should be a mandatory gift for everyone's fiftieth birthday!"
  - **Buck Matthews, WBLV-FM**
    Twin Lake, Michigan

Books by Robert O. Redd

How to Conduct an Energy Audit

published by amacom

Achievers Never Quit, How to Create a Life Plan for the Years After 50

published by Thornapple Publishing Company

WHIMSEY, WIT AND WISDOM

FOR THE WONDERFUL YEARS AFTER FIFTY

Ann Redd • Robert Redd

The Thornapple Publishing Company

FOR INFORMATION, ADDRESS:
THE THORNAPPLE PUBLISHING COMPANY
P.O. BOX 256
ADA, MICHIGAN, 49301

LIBRARY OF CONGRESS CATALOGING IN:
• RETIREMENT PLANNING
• HUMOR
• FAMILY RELATIONS
• HOW TO
PUBLICATION DATA:
•HUMOR AND LIFESTYLES
•REDD, ROBERT O. AND ANN
•WHIMSEY, WIT AND WISDOM,
    FOR THE WONDERFUL YEARS AFTER FIFTY
LIBRARY OF CONGRESS CATALOG CARD NUMBER:
90-090119

ISBN 1-877756-03-2

First Printing: 1990
Second Printing: 1995

THAT WONDERFUL GIFT: HUMOR

Humor never leaves us. It is a gift from our Creator that provides perspective at every age and in every circumstance, even to the final moment of life!

Here's to the wonderful years after fifty–the children are raised, we are feeling great, the mortgage is paid off. Now we can do what we have always wanted to do . . . **whatever that was?**

Keep your sense of humor bright. That's the only thing you may have to take with you when the years after fifty are over.

DEDICATION

We dedicate this book to Bob's father, Otto B. Redd, who never lost his sense of humor, no matter **what** . . . and to our children, who tolerate our sense of humor no matter **what**.

Ann and Bob Redd

Acknowledgements

This book reflects the helpful advice of Gloria Slykhouse, the editor of "Choices," a senior's magazine, where many of the articles in the book first appeared in a slightly different form.

The helpful editorial assistance of Gus Covello and Marsha Redd is reflected in the quality of the manuscript.

Much thanks is due to Louise Bauer, the artist who created the cover and to Bernard Nash, former Executive Director of AARP, Lawrence Webster, Mac Johnson, Dr. Donald Holmes, Mary Kathryn Wallace, Jack Harper, Doris Blough, Jack Hogan, James Mahoy, and Buck Matthews for their helpful comments after reading the manuscript.

Articles were written by Bob except where attributed to Ann.

TABLE OF CONTENTS

**CHAPTER 1   TRANSITIONS AND
MATTERS OF IMPORTANCE   13**

Whether it be outplacement or retirement, the need for perspective is essential to a smooth life change. It may be tougher than you think!

**CHAPTER 2   SPOUSES, LOUSES AND
OTHER SIGNIFICANT RELATIONSHIPS   32**

No one is perfect! But some are better than others.

**CHAPTER 3   TRAVEL (IT'S HARDER
TO HIT A MOVING TARGET)   71**

After 40 years staring out the window and longing for freedom, you have arrived. Vacation, 365 days a year and no responsibilities (for some it may be a little boring).

**CHAPTER 4   LIVING WITH PURPOSE:
IT'S LATER THAN YOU THINK!   85**

Time flies when you do what you want, when you want, and nobody tells you how to do it —except your spouse!

INDEX OF ARTICLES   115

INTRODUCTION

People living in the twentieth century have witnessed enormous change. In less than 100 years mankind has evolved from a horse and buggy society to space age technology.

Life expectancy has increased from 40 in 1900 to nearly 80 in 1990, but more important, the "functional" age . . . the measure of a person's ability to live a vitalized life has expanded to within a few years of the end.

A lifetime can now be thought of as being divided into roughly four quarters.

• The first 25 years are devoted to learning and launching a first career.

• A second period follows until 50 or 55. Marriage is consummated, children are raised, and several career changes are completed for both spouses.

• The third quarter of life brings the prime year—healthy, exciting years offering opportunities to use the skills and experience accumulated over five decades or more.

- Phase four . . . slow down. But again, individuals are very different. For some this retrenchment comes as early as 65 and for others as late as 90.

This book focuses on the creative possibilities of the exciting third quarter of life. Medical technology has presented millions of people with the opportunity to have 20 to 30 vitalized years–but the myths about life after 50, 60, 70 must change!

This is not a time to withdraw into a life of leisure. It is a time to grow and fulfill our full potential. It is a time to give back to society the wisdom and skills that we have been blessed with.

It is a time to discover latent talents, to mold young minds, to leave a legacy of hope for future generations. The only limits are a person's imagination and courage.

The columns and cartoons enclosed provide some hints of what you may experience after 50 and some fun-filled anecdotes to stimulate your creativity.

CHAPTER 1

TRANSITIONS AND OTHER MATTERS OF IMPORTANCE

"NOBODY SAID IT WOULD BE EASY."

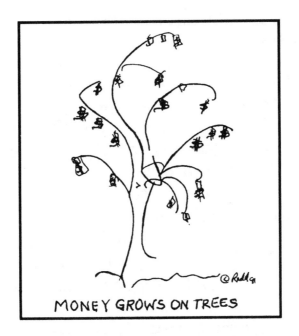

MONEY GROWS ON TREES

THE EXPERTS SAY:

PLAN FOR FINANCIAL SECURITY WITH STOCKS AND BONDS. IT'S A GOOD IDEA TO EARN A FEW DOLLARS WORKING, JUST TO KEEP AHEAD OF INFLATION.

ADVICE FROM AUNT ANN :

DON'T DO ANYTHING YOU WON'T ENJOY, WHETHER FOR PAY OR AS A VOLUNTEER. THE GREATEST PAYBACKS FOR BEING INVOLVED ARE KINSHIP AND A SENSE OF ACCOMPLISHMENT.

MONEY SEEMS TO SPROUT FROM SEEDS OF LOVE THAT WE PLANT IN THE LIVES OF OTHERS. IN A WAY, MONEY "GROWS ON TREES."

SMOOTH TRANSITION? IT ALL DEPENDS ...

The transition from a full-time working career to the unknown of "retirement" is often a difficult task. Somehow we have to find a new orientation and view life from a different perspective. Humor can help answer this challenge.

"Why is retirement wasted on old people?" asked one of my son's friends when I told him I was planning to retire. I thought, *"Some nerve. Who's old? Furthermore, that kid will never retire. The way he drives, he will be lucky to make it to 30."*

Many people think the years after full time employment are the front door to the nursing home or the back door to the "life of Riley"– sleeping late, playing golf, traveling to a condo on the beach in the winter, and never having a care in the world.

Most men and woman find the retirement adjustment very much like getting married–a major change in life style and in many relationships, with more time and less money to spend. But most of all, it's "different life styles for different folks."

Some "retire" like baseball players, starting new careers. Others hit the road in an RV. One of our friends started his own home-based business–making and selling children's wooden jigsaw puzzles. As you cruise through the pages of these writings, we hope you will embrace the joyful side of life after 50.

If you are new to the idea of retirement, you might discover a fresh idea or two; if you are an old hand, we hope you will chuckle with us.

WHAT'S IMPORTANT

"Jack and I just passed forty. We can't believe it! And we don't even have an IRA, or Keogh, or even a Christmas Club Savings. What will happen to us when we retire?"

Jane, my next door neighbor, was in "panicsville"---children in high school and middle school, and the prospect of six to ten years of college tuition for their four children. Will there be anything left to support their "golden years"?

I assured her that it would all work out. After all, Ann and I had made it. We were alive and financially well. It's simple. All you need is rich relatives, or an oil well on the "back forty," or a winning ticket in the lottery, or lots of luck on the job! We had good luck.

We make no assurances that you will discover how to attain financial security within the pages of this "tome." On the other hand, you just might. And besides, money is not the central issue of life after fifty, believe it or not.

Well being is not assured by possessing wealth, even though there are thousands of financial planners, insurance salesmen, stock brokers and sundry others–some with questionable credentials–advising folks how to invest to assure happiness and monetary security after retirement.

The facts are, you will have plenty of money to live on if you plan your lifelong career properly, but you will never have enough money if you depend on it for security.

"What is a lifelong career plan, and where can I get one?" you might ask. Read on. You may find some answers in this book, but you must develop your own unique ways of finding happiness after 50.

HELP IS NEAR

THE EXPERTS SAY:

LEAVE YOUR DESK CLEAN, AND HELP YOUR REPLACEMENT UNDERSTAND HOW YOU DID THE JOB.

ADVICE FROM UNCLE BOB:

YOU MAY WANT TO SHRED SOME OF THE LETTERS YOU WROTE. BE SMART LIKE THE INDIANS. THEY ALWAYS COVERED THEIR TRAIL!

DON'T BE SURPRISED IF YOUR SUCCESSOR DOES NOT ASK YOU FOR ADVICE. YOU HAVE ALREADY BEEN IDENTIFIED AS THE PERSON TO BE BLAMED FOR ALL THE EXISTING PROBLEMS–AND MANY THAT WILL OCCUR IN THE FUTURE!

"GOING–TO–BE'S"

There is a book shop in St. Michaels, Maryland. It's in an ancient building converted from a home. The proprietor is a very old woman with great intellect, who collects and sells special books that she has searched out for her shop. As a pastime, she prints unusual quotations around the ceiling line of her salesroom.

One of her quotations is, "You can't tell a book by its cover and you can't tell a person by his appearance." That line of words printed on the walls has been etched in my mind since our visit.

It came to have new meaning last week when we visited Ann's 45th high school class reunion. My first impression as we entered the meeting hall was, *"There are quite a few old people here. What am I doing here?"* Most were 63, but appeared older. Three wars, job pressures, and countless struggles with children had taken a heavy toll. The lines etched in their faces told the story of their experiences.

We crunched potato chips and talked about World War II, how we built our first homes, what the children were doing.

Some told about their new jobs—working as Red Cross volunteers, selling cars or delivering flowers. Everyone seemed busy Suddenly, I realized that these people were not "old folks." They were interesting, vital citizens involved in their communities, using their experience, contributing to the well-being of friends, family and others in their communities.

As I reflected after the meeting, I was reminded of my grandmother, who taught me to read, to play euchre, and to seed cherries; of my favorite uncle, who helped me rebuild a bicycle; and my grandfather, who had endless energy.

It's not a matter of age or appearance after all! You can't tell a book by its cover, and you can't tell a person by his appearance." People over 50 are not has-beens, they are **going-to-be's!**

NUTRITION OR ATTRITION?

THE EXPERTS SAY:

EAT RIGHT, LOSE WEIGHT, LOWER YOUR CHOLESTEROL, AND AVOID SALT AND SUGAR.

ADVICE FROM AUNT ANN:

COMPROMISE: JUST EAT ONCE A DAY, AND SPEND THE REST OF THE TIME PLANNING THE MENU FOR THE NEXT DAY!

PERHAPS WE MIGHT JUST EAT WHAT WE LIKE. BOB'S GRANDMOTHER ATE EGGS, BACON, PORK CHOPS AND COOKED WITH LARD. SHE LIVED TO THE AGE OF 102! THAT'S LONG ENOUGH.

"MORE SO"

Occasionally a pearl of wisdom is revealed in the murky waters of life. An incisive insight came to my attention recently in Dr. Ken Dychtwalds book *Agewave*.. He related a comment by an "older woman" in his retirement planning class. She explained aging in two words,"More So," and she went on to say that as we grow older we become "more so" in every way. Good and bad traits amplify.

What a marvelously simple truth! Gerontologists have observed for years that as persons age they seem to be less alike; each person expresses his or her own unique gifts. Lifestyles become more diverse—some take off to join the Peace Corps, others continue working, and some sit in a big chair watching television. Few need to conform to peer pressures, so they do what they like.

Of course, we all know a few grouches who spit on the sidewalk, kick cats and rage at the government, and some of those "more so" folks are only thirty years old. In fact, some of the saddest people I ever met in my consulting career were young "old" men or women, who took themselves so seriously that they were a bore to be with.

How wonderful it is to be "more so" in a positive way and to have the time to pursue those special causes that reflect our values and interests—teaching adults literacy, singing in a choir, raising flowers, hiking in the Rockies, selling soap, reading to the blind . . . the list is endless.

Remember those high school cheers? Let's invent our own over 50 cheer . . . **"Go get 'em Tigers . . . Be More So!"**

THERE IS GOOD NEWS AND BAD NEWS

THE EXPERTS SAY:

HAVE A PHYSICAL EXAM EVERY YEAR.
THERE IS MORE CHANCE FOR SURVIVAL IF
A SERIOUS DISEASE IS DIAGNOSED AND
TREATED EARLY.

ADVICE FROM UNCLE BOB:

GET A SECOND OPINION IF THE SUGGESTED
PROCEDURE COSTS MORE THAN $12.
IT MAY BE A REVENUE ENHANCEMENT
PROGRAM FOR THE PHYSICIAN!

EXERT EVERY EFFORT TO STAY WELL AND
OUT OF THE HOSPITAL. MORE PEOPLE DIE
IN HOSPITALS THAN IN ANY OTHER PLACE.

WHAT YOU WILL BE IS WHAT YOU WERE

Last month I had the pleasure of leading a discussion on retirement planning for the eighth graders at a middle school. Age fourteen may seem a little early to start thinking about retirement, but it is not!

The session opened with an invitation to the students to ask questions. The first was from a skinny, blue-eyed rascal in the front row.

"Do you miss your hair?" he queried.

I gasped and assured him that it was "just thinning on top." The next question was just as formidable.

"Do you have false teeth?"

Obviously these kids had a distorted view of "old folks"–anyone over eighteen, that is. I quickly launched into a more formal approach to the dialogue, which led them through ten keys to happy retirement, based on the recognition that how you look, feel, and live at 60 will depend on what you do from now until then. (This even applies to a 60-year-old looking forward to 90).

1. EAT PROPERLY. Grandma always told me, "You are what you eat." She lived to be 102, so that proves it worked for her.

2. EXERCISE REGULARLY. Get your heart rate up 25 percent for 20 minutes, at least three times a week.

3. THINK SAFETY. Fasten the car seat belt, stay away from firearms if you haven't been trained, cross streets at the crosswalks, and avoid sky diving, especially if you don't have a parachute.

4. RELAX AND SLEEP. Stress is the root cause for 75 percent of illness. Relaxation techniques can replace most medication and can even reduce chronic pain and hypertension.

5. MAINTAIN A POSITIVE ATTITUDE. There are countless challenges that at first seem to be insurmountable. It's courage that counts in the long run

6. CONTINUE TO DISCOVER. The greatest joy and most rewarding activity in life is learning, whether in school, on the job, reading a book, or just being with a friend.

7. SET GOALS. Purpose, aspiration, motivation, hope, a reason for living, all emanate from the direction toward which we point our lives through clearly defined objectives.

8. AVOID DRUGS. The wisdom of the body is sufficient. We only need to permit it to lead. Alcohol, tobacco, cocaine, librium, and caffeine all distort the natural processes and increase the pace of aging.

9. SET STANDARDS. Your convictions about "what is right and wrong" and your adherence to those beliefs are the most important keys to a long and successful life.

10. BE HUMBLE. Success is never final. A view of the stars on a clear night affirms the magnificence of the mystery that our Creator has wrought and gives perspective to our lives and concerns.

I survived the memorable challenge of the eighth grader inquisition and hope some of my suggestions were accepted.

But to tell the truth, they were probably more impressed by my claims of being a weekly attendee at the roller skating rink than by the profound truths I tried to explain. After all, how many 64-year-old's still "jive on the wheels?"

Now that I think about it, I started roller skating when I was fourteen at a junior high outing. So in many respects, **what I am now is what I have been.**

CHAPTER 2

SPOUSES, LOUSES AND OTHER SIGNIFICANT RELATIONSHIPS

THE EXPERTS SAY:

BE PATIENT WHEN YOUR WIFE IS TOO BUSY TO FIX YOUR LUNCH. IT DOES NOT NECESSARILY MEAN SHE DISLIKES YOU.

ADVICE FROM UNCLE BOB:

LEARN TO COOK.

YOUR WIFE REDIRECTED HER LIFE 20 YEARS AGO, AND SHE HAS NUMEROUS SOCIAL COMMITMENTS MORE URGENT THAN YOUR LUNCH.

SHE MAY BECOME MORE RESPONSIVE TO YOUR NEEDS IF YOU INVITE A YOUNG NEIGHBOR LADY IN TO HELP YOU MASTER THE CULINARY ARTS!

BUT NOT FOR LUNCH

"For better or worse but not for lunch." That's what she said before I retired, and I guess I really did not understand. I did not know my wife had a full agenda during the day. I thought she would be available, and even anxious, to go places with me whenever I wanted her to. The first month I got her spices alphabetized, reorganized the laundry room, and set up new policies regarding the disposal of the newspapers. But she never had time to go to the lumber yard with me.

After doing some research, I discovered there is not much written about the wife's adjustment to retirement, so I asked Ann how she felt. Here are some of her comments:

"There is something missing! No one is talking about the wife's part in all of this retirement planning. What am I to do? After 30 or 40 years of marriage, with the husband going to work, what do I have to do to accommodate this invasion into my domain? The dishwasher is running at the same time as the washing

machine. That isn't the way I do it! I feel guilty every time I go to a meeting and leave Bob sitting at home.

'ARE YOU GOING OUT AGAIN TODAY?' he asks. 'WHERE ARE YOU GOING?'

"I never had to answer those kinds of questions before!"

Those are just a few choice words from my wife. She is absolutely right! The important keys to life after 50 are communication, a willingness to adjust, time planning that provides for each of the spouses to have a sense of independence, and a place for your things.

A final few words from Ann.

"Here we are again, just like we were before the children came. We now have time to do what we really wanted to do. But have those things been lost amid the diapers, diplomas, weddings, and now the grandchildren?

"Compromises have to be negotiated. There must be a willingness to share fears, doubts and expectations with each other.

"At this time in our lives, the best tool we have is our sense of humor. Time will take care of most of the problems, and, someday, when I hear the front door close in the middle of the day, I will immediately know it's not a burglar . . . it's just Bob coming home!"

IS THERE ROMANCE AFTER 50?

At fourteen, "romance" was a steamy word that caused my knees to weaken. I yearned to say, "Hi Margie" to an unapproachable, teenage "light of my life" . . . but the words froze in my throat. Fifty years have passed, and I still have lots of confusion about "romance."

My thesaurus indicates that romance has many meanings–intimacy, involvement, companionship, closeness – a nice word to describe warm feelings and enthusiasm. But in our high-speed, high-tech age, no one seems to have time for these refinements. The omnipotent TV screen has bundled all forms of affection into sexual affairs, all fear into terror, all encounters into drug busting, and all anger into violence. Thoughts are converted into emotions and then into action in eight minute segments punctuated with sensory flashes of commercial appeals designed to drive you into a frenzy of desire . . . for whatever.

Where has involvement and romance gone? What about the long walks in the woods, warm embraces in front of the fireplace, a sip of iced tea while rocking on the front porch together? Perhaps it is time for a rediscovery of these finer aspects of life.

I propose we organize a "Society for the Preservation and Promotion of Romance in America" SPPRA. No heavy breathing, no performance anxiety, just warm words of kindness in a world gone wild with change and greed. We could distribute song books listing old favorites like "Tell Me Why," "Let Me Call You Sweetheart," "My Buddy." We might even influence song writers to compose music that has a melody!

Romance doesn't stop there. A broader meaning of the word romance is "to captivate," "to enthrall," "to lure." This sense of adventure was expressed eloquently in Richard Halliburton's book, *The Royal Road to Romance*. He described the excitement he felt as he traveled around the world. Romance can reflect our zest for life in numerous ways.

Many persons have dedicated their energies and time to romances much broader than intimate relationships. They participate in activities that enrich the lives of others or themselves in their own creative ventures–learning to fly an airplane, writing poetry, helping at a hospice, or going to an Elderhostel in Sweden.

We can discover the reality and joy of living our own lives to the fullest with "romance." Be it a pursuit of your chosen imaginative expressions, searching out new experiences, or sharing the companionship of a loved one, the enthusiasm we devote to these undertakings adds vitality to our lives and to every one we meet.

WIFE–TIME SECRETS

"It's Sunday night and time to review our weekly calendars," I shouted over the din of the TV set.

"Can't do it now. I'm watching "Murder She Wrote," Ann replied.

My wife is an avid murder mystery fan. She schedules our meals and social commitments around murder programs. She started this passionate interest shortly after I retired. I'm not sure if it's just an escape from boredom or if she is trying to find a neat way to do me in.

Shortly after I retired, we discovered that we had an urgent need to "check signals" about where we were planning to go. It was especially urgent to resolve plans when Ann was going to be away at lunch time, so I would not starve. Much to my amazement, she felt no guilt for leaving me to fix my own lunch. After several heated discussions about confused schedules, we agreed to have a meeting at the kitchen table every Sunday night to review calendars.

At first, Ann was a little secretive. She would say, "I'm going to be 'out' Wednesday afternoon."

"Where?" I'd ask.

"Oh, just downtown," she'd whisper.

"But where?" I'd repeat.

I don't ask for too many details now. I have finally realized that wives need to have private time, and it's not necessary that I know that she is going to the shoe store for the fourth time this month. "Shop 'till you drop" is her life challenge.

Our discussions and the calendar help us both know when we can do things together and greatly facilitate communication, which is one of the most important skills couples need to develop after retirement. We have learned to resolve differences and negotiate compromises by developing a sense of trust and goodwill.

These are very important qualities to cultivate at any time in a marriage, but it is especially important if you both decide to retire (and remain married).

WHEN WILL YOU BE BACK?

When will you be back? Where will you eat lunch? Who's going with you? Ann decided to go to a Garden Club meeting on Monday, and I checked out all of the details before she left.

Prior to retirement, this was not possible . . . or even of interest. She went about her activities with practically no surveillance. Now she has more attention than she needs or even wants.

When she buys new shoes, I know it. When she writes to her sister, I know it. I know everything she eats every day. This is the togetherness that our new life style has provided.

She talks about getting a part-time job or visiting her cousin in Arizona without me! It's incredible how things have changed. She never mentioned her cousin in Arizona before I retired. She sometimes says she feels guilty when she is away from me doing something she likes to do. I don't understand that.

Perhaps I should buy an RV, and we could travel all over the country, and then we could stop in Arizona. Or we could sign up for a tournament bridge series in Atlanta. I try to plan what we could do, but I have noticed that it usually works better if I talk with her before plans are finalized.

Maybe the retirement adjustment has something to do with communication. Talking things over and reaching agreements is probably a better way. Fortunately, Ann has a sense of humor and ignores me most of the time.

It appears that it would be better to plan ahead. Attending a retirement planning program three to five years before the event could be helpful. The programs present the issues and challenges so that participants begin to think about important decisions that they must make in the future.

Where will we live? Will we be snowbirds? How much money will we have and need? How will we spend our time? What activities are of mutual interest? How will we maintain a strong sense of self-esteem?

It's like building a house or planning a career change. The better the pre-planning, the better the final result.

I just heard the car come into the garage. I wonder what Ann brought me TODAY.

"DANCING" @ Redd 90

THE EXPERTS SAY:

GO DANCING AT LEAST ONCE A MONTH (WITH YOUR SPOUSE).

ADVICE FROM UNCLE BOB:

REMEMBER THOSE DAYS OF THE PAST GLORY WHEN YOU DANCED ALL NIGHT? WELL, THEY ARE PAST!

BE CAUTIOUS ABOUT SWING, THE TWIST AND JITTER-BUGGING. YOUR MIND CAN MAKE COMMITMENTS YOUR BODY CAN'T DELIVER.

TAKE AN ASPIRIN WHEN YOU GET HOME. IT WILL EASE YOUR JOINT PAIN AND DIMINISH THE THROBBING IN YOUR HEAD.

FUN AND GAMES WE PLAY

As the months have passed since retirement, I have made many discoveries— some major ones, such as the joy of getting up in the morning when I want to, and others that are more subtle.

The most recent discovery came to full awareness last weekend. I was burning the dried leaves and branches that were left after a large oak tree was cut down in our back yard. The fire was burning with remarkable intensity.

Suddenly, Ann sprayed the flames with water. That was the moment that I made the discovery! My wife is a "counter-action operator." She does just the opposite of the most expected behavior in an effort to balance my actions. Of course, she had a valid basis for concern since I had spiced the fire with gasoline.

My first inkling of her counter-action tendencies came earlier this summer. She put a large coffee can in my car with matches, a Hershey bar, and two candles.

"Why," I asked,"do I need this in the summer . . . in the winter, OK, but why in the summer?"

She replied, "Your car may break down, and you can eat the Hershey bar until help comes."

"Fine, but what do I do with the candles?"

"If it's dark, you can put them on the road to warn oncoming cars!"

I am watched over in many ways. Ann always ties red flags on things sticking out of the car windows, even if they are only eight inches long. She warns me when I drive left of center and won't let me push the grocery cart because, she says, I'm too reckless.

I suspect my wife might tell you, if she had the chance, that there are some things I do that may not reflect careful contemplation. Her efforts are all for my own good. So I just accept her "counter-action programs" with patience and love.

MATTERS OF THE HEART

Whenever we visit our children, we notice they are doing things differently than we would have done them. One son is educating his children at home."All the way through high school," he says, although he just started this year. My daughter plans to have her next child at home with a midwife in attendance. And my youngest son just started sky diving.

Ann and I often talk about these "strange" departures from the conventional approaches that we followed in the 1940's and 1950's. We learned the facts of life watching Mickey Rooney and Judy Garland in the Andy Hardy movies. "It's all different now," my children tell me. "We're living in a society inundated with drugs and discord. 30 percent of the children in the schools are from divorced families."

I must admit things are different, and sometimes my advice seems to fit a time when values didn't change so fast. Grandparents need to be cautious about offering recommendations.

Generally, issues divide into two

categories: problems of the mind, such as "What will happen to the stock market next year?" or "Is it too late to plant tulip bulbs?"– or problems of the heart, like my son asking, "Should I marry Alice, the girl I met in my karate class last month?" or "Will you lend me $40,000 to buy the house on Brandon Street that we really love?"

Matters of the mind are handled promptly with direct, decisive answers. Matters of the heart, however, require careful consideration and measured responses. We listen to their problems, but they must resolve the trade-offs and make their own decisions.

Financial support is one of the toughest issues. The resources we have accumulated must support us for many years. We will not be able to add much to these reserves. We take a firm position, and then help them develop a sound money management plan. We want to be supportive and guide our children toward becoming independent and self-sufficient.

GRANDPA'S LITTLE BUDDY

THE EXPERTS SAY:

GRANDCHILDREN ARE AN ENDLESS JOY. SPEND AS MUCH TIME AS POSSIBLE WITH THEM.

ADVICE FROM UNCLE BOB:

BE CAREFUL WHAT YOU SAY TO THEM. CHILDREN NEVER FORGET A PROMISE!

TRY TO REMAIN WITHIN SHOUTING DISTANCE OF THE PARENTS IF YOU ARE OUTNUMBERED.

BE WARY. GRANDCHILDREN ARE LIKE DEAD FISH. AFTER THREE DAYS THEY BEGIN TO SMELL. . . . LITTLE ONES START TO SMELL SOONER THAN THAT.

"GRAND" PARENTING

It takes skill, intelligence, and judgment to walk the fine line of being a "grand" parent. Of course, the "grand" children view us as allies with a common enemy—their parents. And it's easy to win their loyalty with cookies and lots of hugs.

But their parents, our children, represent the tougher challenge: How to be supportive; but not bossy; how to see them make mistakes, but not interfere; how to know the answers, and not tell.

Being a grandparent is both an art and a science. It's the art of knowing what to say and how to say it. It's the science of knowing ourselves, knowing our prejudices and emotional needs; knowing when we are more selfish than loving, more fearful than brave, more critical than kind.

We are not taught in school "How to be grandparents," so we perform mostly by trial and error. For example, Jim and Alice, our neighbors, faced a new challenge three years after they retired. Their daughter, Margie, moved back home with her two boys, one seven and the other ten years old. They were typical boys, full of energy and curiosity. They did the usual "naughty" things. In one week, they broke three windows in the neighborhood with a new BB gun. Jim replaced the windows and made peace with the neighbors. To say that his life had changed was a gross understatement, but he seems to have found a new "lease on life."

He told me, "I know I may only have ten or so years left, but I can't imagine a more useful way to spend them than helping my daughter with the boys." It's a matter of attitude . . . a "being" attitude" that encourages involvement with others and produces love, courage and hope.

We believe our society will soon recognize the value of nurturing grandparents.**They are one of our nation's great natural resources.**

STORY TELLING TIME © Rudd 90

NEVER DROP A NEIGHBOR'S PIANO
(ON YOUR FOOT)

THE EXPERTS SAY :

BE HELPFUL TO YOUR NEIGHBOR. A FRIEND
IN NEED IS A FRIEND INDEED.

ADVICE FROM AUNT ANN:

OFFER TIME AND CONCERN, BUT DO NOT
LEND MONEY OR GIVE UNREQUESTED
ADVICE.

ALWAYS STAY IN TOUCH WITH OLD FRIENDS.
THEY WILL ENJOY THE LOVE AND CONCERN
YOUR CONTACTS EXPRESS.

FOR THE BEST OF FUTURES

"Help us build a tree house, Grandpa." That was the first thing I heard when I stepped out of the car at my daughter's home. Three boys and a tomboy called "Ruth" swept down upon me with this fervent appeal. That day I worked harder than I had worked in years. It wasn't fair to build just one tree house for all. So we, the four kids and I, built four tree houses. They are monuments that will be remembered forever in the minds of delighted grandchildren.

It reminded me that we have so much to share with young people and even our middle-aged children. Some sociologists would like us to believe that there is a wall rising between the generations. What a tragedy if this should ever happen!

The young people need us and we need them. So I've started a program of bridge building in our family. We, who have lived for 60, 70, 80 years, have much to relate. Let's get busy spreading our mind power to others.

• **Tell them** how it was in the old days: where we worked, how we met our mate, where we went on vacation, and what our grandparents were like.

• **Show them** how to crochet a pot holder or how to play Canasta (a card game with hundreds of cards, if you don't remember) or how to build a bird feeder.

• **Assure them** that they will survive the problems that seem so difficult, and that the most important attribute they can cultivate is a sense of humor.

We grew up in a slower time when people flourished by reading good books and vibrated to songs that had a melody. Maybe the kids would enjoy hearing your favorite Glenn Miller records while there are still machines to play them on.

We can be mentors to those who need guidance, teachers to those who need skills, courage to those who need hope and love to those who are lonely. **Here's to the best of futures for all.**

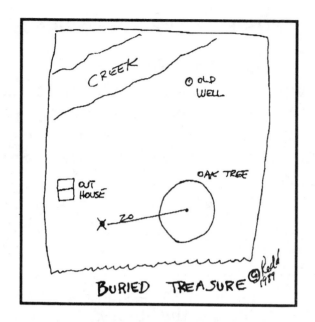

THE EXPERTS SAY:

"RATHER SAFE THAN SORRY."
KEEP YOUR ASSETS IN A SECURE
PLACE: A BANK? A SAVINGS & LOAN?

ADVICE FROM UNCLE BOB:

IF YOU ARE CONCERNED ABOUT THE SAFETY
OF YOUR SAVINGS, BURY SOME OF IT IN A
GLASS JAR IN THE BACKYARD; THEN MAKE A
MAP AND HIDE IT (BE SURE TO REMEMBER
WHERE YOU PUT THE MAP!)

THIS WILL BE A CHALLENGE FOR THE KIDS
AFTER YOU ARE GONE. VEILED REFERENCE
TO THE "MONEY JAR" WILL MAINTAIN YOUR
CHILDREN'S INQUISITIVENESS AND ASSURE
VISITS FOR MANY YEARS.

POSSESSED BY POSSESSIONS

"I don't care what you say. I'm not going to live another week with 14 boxes of books in the bedroom!" commented a lady across the table from my wife and me at the Shrine Club dance in Sarasota.

It was apparent that she was reading the riot act to her new husband. Naturally, I had to butt in and offer solutions.

"You could have a garage sale or donate them to the library," I suggested.

We had only met the couple 30 minutes before by the coincidence of sitting opposite each other at the long tables adjoining the dance floor.

She explained that they had recently married and merged the households of their former homes. Both had lost a spouse of long tenure and had an irreplaceable collections of memorabilia, furniture, books, pictures, beds, and other items too numerous to mention.

Fortunately, the band started playing and we terminated our marriage counseling session, but it brought to mind the dilemma Ann and I have been struggling with for 35 years.

The first years of our marriage we had very little–a rented house, a few chairs, and a bed. Over the years we bought more. A lifetime accumulation including a house, a cottage, three bicycles, 143 board feet of used lumber, numerous boxes of nails and screws, pipe fittings and a used saxophone.

The bottom line is that the more stuff I have, the more time I spend taking care of it.

When I brought this dilemma to my wife's attention she said, "It's simple. Just get rid of the things you don't need."

Now that sounds easy enough, but how do I know what I will need? Just last summer we used an old window we had stored for 11 years, for the renovation of my son's 60-year-old house, and I put 30 pounds of lime on my garden that had been in the garage since 1976. "Waste not, want not" was the motto of the 1930s! Those commandments from the past, stored in my mind, are impossible to silence.

However, in spite of my inability to resolve this matter for myself, I am recommending to all retirees that they simplify their lives by disposing of any item they have not used during the last three years. Stop wasting time moving things from garage to basement, from house to cottage, and worst of all, from house to house. Have the courage to make those tough decisions. Release yourself from the bondage of serving possessions!

Incidentally, if you have any real good stuff, call me. I'm in the phone directory and I have a truck to haul it away!

MAN'S BEST FRIEND

THE EXPERTS SAY:

ANIMALS ARE LOYAL AND FAITHFUL COMPANIONS. EVERYONE OVER 50 SHOULD SHARE HIS/HER HOME WITH A LOVING PET.

ADVICE FROM AUNT ANN:

DOGS AND CATS SENSE THE NEEDS AND WEAKNESSES OF THE AGED. SOME BREEDS EVEN HOLD THEIR OWNERS HOSTAGE.

I PREFER STUFFED ANIMALS. THEY DON'T EAT MUCH AND NEVER MAKE LOUD NOISES OR COMPLAIN.

WE HAVE GONE TO THE DOGS

The President has addressed many social issues in our nation, but he has completely ignored the insidious encroachment of our civil rights by pets. This matter came to my attention during the Christmas season. Ann decided to buy a dog bed for our eight-year-old, black and tan Doberman, Hedwig.

Hedwig is not a dog you buy a bed for without discussing the choice of designs with her. She is a stubborn, over-weight "hausfrau". Her reaction as we pulled the plastic-filled, canvas bag from the box was unequivocal disapproval. We placed it in her favorite spot right in front of the TV and urged her to climb in. **She refused and refused and refused.**

Since that initial rejection, we have tried various methods to manipulate her onto the bed. One evening I found Ann sitting in the center of the dog bed telling Hedwig how comfortable it was. I took a more direct approach, picking her up and throwing her into the middle.

We removed half of the ground plastic to make it less threatening, sprayed it with perfume, and offered rewards. Nothing works!

Hedwig's domination of the family extends well beyond the new bed. She insists on only the most expensive food, and must have a dog biscuit every time she returns from her tours of the yard. These biscuits, of course, are "completely balanced based on the AAFCO protocol feeding studies and contain vitamins A, C, D, E and wheat germ!" So says the box.

We are not alone in our battle for domestic rights. One of our widow friends has two large dogs and a 25-pound cat who hold her hostage. "Rambo" her 90-pound Irish setter insists on placing his paws on my shoulders and licking my nose whenever I visit the house, in spite of her screaming, "DOWN RAMBO, DOWN BOY, DOWN!"

I have concluded that we have created our own problems by abdicating control. After surviving four wars, raising three children, and struggling through countless family conflicts, it is hard to fight the iron will of house pets. Perhaps it is too much to hope for support from the federal government, but it seems to me this would come under the jurisdiction of the state sociologists concerned about elder abuse. I plan to write the Human Ecology Department in Lansing if Hedwig does not "shape up" soon.

A 25 POUND CAT

© Redd 90

VACATIONS REDEFINED

Last fall will be a time to either remember or try to forget. We were blessed with a family reunion. Three children, seven grandchildren, cats, dogs, and other nameless pets swooped down upon us the first and second weeks of August.

What grandparent can resist the opportunity to share several joy-filled weeks with loving children and grandchildren? After this "experiment," we may be the first!

The event involved three phases: **BEFORE, DURING, AND AFTER.**

Phase I,. **BEFORE:** We tried to safety-proof the house. All firearms, knives, poisons, and inflammables were locked in a fireproof safe. We stocked up on generic brand soda pop and cheap beer. The bed mattresses and sofas were wrapped in waterproof covers, and breakable china was stowed on shelves seven feet from the floor.

It was impossible to predict what happened in Phase II, **DURING:** The tribe rampaged through the house, testing the durability of my VCR and riding my Rupp-rider minibike. Ann spent the weeks in the kitchen, cooking endless meals, while I served as director of floor wrestling and other forms of hand-to-hand combat.

Phase III, **AFTER**: They left with much hugging. There were heaps of photos, many remembrances that will be repeated for decades, and a resolution to do it again when everyone is speaking to each other.

Next summer, Ann and I are going to China or Nicaragua for a peaceful escape from the grind of retirement and the possibility of another family reunion!

"KILL THE UMPIRE!"

SO WHAT'S NEW ABOUT RECYCLING?

The newspapers are full of articles proclaiming the environmental importance of recycling. Save bottles, bundle paper, and donate clothing to charities.

When I was growing up during the depression of the thirties, we had a better phrase for the same activities. It was, "A PENNY SAVED IS A PENNY EARNED."

My cousins and I never saw new clothing. We never figured out who bought the original pants or sweaters. All we knew was they were warm and didn't cost our parents any money. If Mom or Dad tried that now with teenagers, it would start a war!

Then there was the home-made meat loaf. Mother would grind up the leftovers from last week and put it in the new loaf– week after week. The wine makers in Spain call that "Solerno"; it adds to the flavor, I'm told.

Grandpa used the fruit jars left after canning to bottle his illegal gin. We used old papers to stuff around the cracks in the windows, and we gathered coal that had fallen off the railroad cars along the tracks. Kids that smoked often would "shoot snipes." That was the code phrase for picking up cigarettes, snipping off the ends and smoking the butts. Nothing was wasted.

One of my fondest memories was the "clop, clop" of the horse who pulled the rag man's wagon. He would ride along the street shouting, "Rags and old iron . . . rags and old iron." His livelihood came from the things gathered and sold at the scrap yard.

No doubt the environmentalist would be up in arms about the horse manure left on the streets. It never bothered us. We always figured if a person didn't have common sense enough not to step in the manure, that was his problem. Now we have huge government agencies trying to protect folks from their own stupidity!

My uncle repaired push lawn mowers and had a building full of reclaimed cutters, handles, and wheels. He never threw anything away. He would salvage the useable parts from an old mower and resell them. We never bought anything new until we ran out of ways to fix up what we had.

It seems to me that the place to start recycling is by not throwing things into the trash. Fix them up, find new creative uses, and share them with others. My children cringe when I drive up with a trailer full of "heritage gifts."But I assure them that someday they will find a use for a "slightly used" electric water tank, or a bath tub with legs. As I drive away I usually shout, **"A PENNY SAVED IS A PENNY EARNED!"** It gives them something to tell about me after I'm gone.

TREE HOUSES ARE FOR KIDS
(AND GRANDPA'S)

CHAPTER 3

TRAVEL

IT'S HARDER TO HIT A MOVING TARGET

BETTER SAFE THAN SORRY

THE EXPERTS SAY:

BE CAREFUL WHEN DRIVING AFTER DARK OR ON A BUSY HIGHWAY.

ADVICE FROM AUNT ANN:

ALWAYS STAY IN THE LEFT LANE ON FOUR-LANE ROADS SO YOU CAN PASS WITHOUT CHANGING LANES, AND NEVER DRIVE OVER 35 MPH, EVEN ON MAJOR HIGHWAYS.

MEMORIZE THE STATE "EYE" CHART. IT WILL TAKE YEARS FOR THE DRIVER'S LICENSE EXAMINER TO DISCOVER THAT YOU ARE NEARLY BLIND!

SNOW BIRDS

"I'm tired of being cold, shoveling snow, and sliding around on the ice. Next year we are going to Florida for three months," I shouted as I stamped into the living room. It was 15 below zero, we had eight inches of snow on the driveway, and I was mad.

Ann crunched down into her fuzzy wing-back chair and replied, "Yes, but what would you do with your time down there?"

"Well, I would find something to do. They have libraries, golf courses, lots of fishing, and just walking the beach would be fun."

Ann responded like a machine gun. "Two weeks of that, and you would be bored to death. Besides, what about our grandchildren? Where would we stay—and what would I do—and what about my church guild meetings?"

The battle has raged all winter, my second year of retirement. Never before have I had freedom from commitments to a job. If I suffer with aching joints, freezing hands, and frosty ears, IT'S MY FAULT, because IT'S MY CHOICE. No one says to me that I have to stay up north twelve months a year. Freedom is a blessing and a curse. Now I must take responsibility for my own decisions; no one else to blame!

Ann, of course, has a convincing argument. The grandchildren are delightful. She has been involved in group activities for years. It's difficult for her to give up those relationships for an extended stay in another city with just me as a companion. To quote her, "Being with you 24 hours a day is almost too much of a good thing." I am not sure what she means by that.

So we have decided to spend time talking about becoming "snowbirds" next year . . . flying south for the winter. We will need to spend a lot of time discussing alternative locations, but it appears that a compromise is in the making. We agreed that we would not want to miss Christmas with the kids, so we would leave next year after January 15.

We believe having our own place would be better than renting different condos every year, so we may buy. It's going to require several months of negotiation to arrive at a plan that is comfortable for both of us, but that's what marriage is about.

My father-in-law told me, shortly after our wedding, his formula for 40 years of successful marriage. **"Peace at any price!"** I finally understand what he meant.

ESCAPE TO PARADISE ??
(THE FOLLOWING WINTER)

Have you ever dreamed of a month in the sun—the joy of all the time in the world to walk on the beach, sit by the pool, play golf every day? As you stared out of the office window at the ice-covered streets, you imagined in your mind's eye a quiet cottage on the beach, the waves rolling gently over the warm sands, and the pungent aroma of tropical flowers filling the air.

I have news for you . . . three weeks in paradise for achievers is more than enough. If you have seen one palm tree, you have seen them all. And the traffic in those sunbelt cities is worse than Detroit or Los Angeles at 5 P.M.. You can never tell if the drivers are in full control of their faculties, and there is always the nagging fear that some are legally blind!

There are things to do: visit the library try fishing, learn shuffleboard strategy, play golf and walk on the beach; but some of these activities can be very expensive. Business operators plan their pricing to make enough money in three months to pay their expenses and profit for the whole year. Thus, golf costs $20 to $30 per person for 18 holes; fishing costs $35 a day per person, Disneyworld charges $56 admission for a couple. If you are a millionaire, there is no problem; otherwise, you may have to focus on activities at the senior citizens center.

Even sun and blue skies day after day gets boring. "Oh, for just one good old snow storm, pine trees covered with a frosting of crystal white flakes, and a red bird on the feeder."

It's like the time I had a job working in an ice cream parlour. Before I was hired, there never seemed to be enough ice cream to fill my appetite. After three weeks, I was fed up with the mucky stuff.

Have you ever seen a sea gull separated from the flock wandering aimlessly around the beach? In some ways, extended stays in resorts seem that way to my wife and me.

It is difficult to be involved in any meaningful relationships when no one really knows us. Permanent residents say, "If you were going to be here all year, we could use you on several projects" or "Yes, we will be having a program on that subject next July . . . will you be here?"

We huddle together for warmth and socialization and abrade each other until one of us screams for space; then we clear the air with a battle royal and smoke the peace pipe over our key lime pie. When April finally comes, we pack the bags and head back north– tanned, 10 pounds overweight, and full of glowing stories about the wonderful winter we spent in the land of glowing sunsets. **Ann was right after all!**

MOVING DAY!

THE EXPERTS SAY:

THE LARGE HOUSE WAS NEEDED WHEN YOU HAD CHILDREN. NOW IT'S TIME TO CONSOLIDATE, SELL, AND MOVE INTO A CONDO.

ADVICE FROM AUNT ANN:

SORTING THROUGH FORTY YEARS OF ACCUMULATION IS MORE FRIGHTENING THAN AN EARTHQUAKE. JUST BOARD UP THE OLD HOUSE AND LEAVE IT FOR THE HOPEFUL HEIRS.

BUY NEW APPLIANCES, FURNITURE, DISHES, CARPETS, PICTURES . . . THE "WORKS" AND ENJOY THEM WHILE YOU'RE ALIVE AND HEALTHY. IT'S LATER THAN WE THINK!

TO MOVE OR NOT TO MOVE? . . . THAT IS THE QUESTION ?

Sunshine three days in a row. Can there be any doubt spring has arrived in Michigan? Setbacks can be expected. After all, we've had 40-degree days in July. But the worst of winter has passed, and it's now the glory of the "growing season."

The trouble is, everything is growing, and I am growing older. The weeds seem to be stronger than in years past. I pulled at a dead milk weed for nearly ten minutes. It didn't move an inch. Then the contest got serious . . . shovel, pick, strong words . . . and the remnants of the brown monster are scattered around the battleground.

I marched into the house and told Ann, "We are moving out of this house. I spend too much of my valuable time picking up the yard, cutting grass, painting trim, fighting dandelions, cleaning out roof gutters, and repairing fences!"

Ann looked up from her rug hooking and said, "You have mud on your shoes."

Several of our friends have moved into condos and claim it is the best of all worlds. Advantages they list are impressive: security, friendly neighbors, predictable housing costs, activity programs, and no yard or house maintenance.

On the other hand, home ownership has its pluses: a limitless number of pets,("Hedwig" is a constant source of joy) exercise, privacy, and free flowers.

Every year we go through a period of soul searching. Should we stay in the old homestead or move to smaller quarters? The children are terrorized with the prospect of our selling the old homestead, "with all those wonderful memories."

And there is the question of what would happen to our social relationships. We would be leaving our wonderful neighbors. If we move far, we would need to find a new doctor, dentist, and church. Then there is the mortgage shock for the new place, and the condo management association with all their rules!

I guess we will put off the decision about moving for another year and just blacktop the back yard.

MOVING TO ARIZONA

"I could not believe that Carl did that."

"Did what?" Ann asked.

"He is moving to Arizona in November." Carl is my neighbor. He retired in June and took the usual post-retirement trip. He and his wife rented a travel trailer and drove to Tucson. They were there six weeks and returned to tell us that they loved Arizona.

"Never saw anything like it—just sun and sky; you can play golf year round, and it's the fastest growing area in the U. S. of A," Carl boasted. I was surprised at Carl's enthusiasm about another state because he always seemed to enjoy Michigan. He was active in his church and did a lot of cross-country skiing.

That was two weeks ago. Now Carl and his wife, Grace, are now packing up to move to Arizona. They sold their house in three days.

It all may work out "okay," but the odds are against them. They are the third couple I have known that have sold their home and moved within the first year of retirement. The other two are back in their home town, with a lot less money and much more experience.

Sociologists who have studied the adjustments experienced after retirement urge people to "stay put" for the first two years. If retirees want to try a new community, experts suggest that they lease a house for a year and see how they like the new situation. Will they miss their old friends and family? Is the climate comfortable year round? Are there things of interest to do?

Ann suggested I better not tell Carl and Grace about the other couples that came back because it would upset them. I guess I will wait until they return, and then tell them!

THE BIG TRIP

THE EXPERTS SAY:

SHORTLY AFTER RETIRING, YOU ARE EXPECTED TO TRAVEL TO AN EXCITING RESORT FOR A SIX-MONTH VACATION.

ADVICE FROM UNCLE BOB:

PLAN YOUR TRIP SO YOU WILL FULFILL THE HOPES AND DREAMS OF YOUR FRIENDS AND RELATIVES WHO HAVE INVITED YOU TO "COME SEE THEM" ON EVERY CHRISTMAS CARD SINCE 1945.

BE SURE TO TAKE THE DOGS. EVERYONE LOVES YOUR PIT BULLS, "BEAUTY" AND "THE BEAST!"

CHAPTER 4

LIVING WITH PURPOSE

IT'S LATER THAN
YOU THINK!

A HEALTHY HIKE © Redd 90

THE EXPERTS SAY:

HIKING IS AN IDEAL WAY TO ENJOY THE FRESH AIR AND EXPERIENCE INVIGORATING EXERCISE

ADVICE FROM AUNT ANN:

ALWAYS SELECT PATHS THAT ARE DOWN-HILL, SMOOTH, AND HAVE COMFORTABLE RESTROOMS EVERY HALF MILE.

WEAR COMFORTABLE SHOES. CARRY A CHANGE OF SOCKS AND UNDERWEAR IN CASE OF EMERGENCIES.

STAY NEAR THE FRONT OF THE LINE SO YOU WILL NOT BE ASKED TO CARRY ANY FELLOW HIKERS!

THE SECRETS OF A LONG, JOYFUL LIFE

The years after fifty can be the "best years of your life" or "dark gray downers." It's up to you. Careful planning and positive action in three key areas will make the difference.

Unfortunately, many people in our materialistic society believe the answers to life at all ages 40, 50, 60, and beyond– lie in MONEY!

"If I got enough dough, I can handle anything," claimed a 55-year-old, in response to my question, "What are you planning to do during the years after retirement?" Two years later I learned he had been told he only had a year to live.

If it is not money, then what is the answer? The heart of the matter lies in careful balanced attention to the three basic elements of life: Body, Mind, and Spirit.

BODY

We are all mortal, whether we want to accept that consciously, or not. The aging process proceeds more rapidly for some than for others. But all of us face the relentless passage of time. We can significantly influence the rate of aging in four important ways.

Exercise Three times per week, raise the pulse rate 25 percent for at least 20 minutes.

Nutrition Knowledgeable selection of health-supporting foods and careful avoidance of destructive choices.

Awareness Monitoring the body performance in relation to known criteria: blood pressure, heart rate, cholesterol . . .

Serenity Stress reduction routines performed intermittently during the waking day, when distress is sensed.

MIND

Have you ever taken a long, auto trip alone, never speaking to anyone for hours, perhaps days? Then a need arises to communicate. The words seem to hang in the throat . . . the voice sounds strange. The same is true of all mental functions. The mind, like the heart, thrives on activity.

Learning Keeping the growing edge of the senses alive through exposure to new ideas, new people, new places.

Communicating Sharpening the ability to speak, listen, and empathize with other people at all levels of society.

Creating Discovering new combinations of thought and substance that expand your universe and contribute to the ongoing progress of mankind

SPIRIT

Elan vital: Is the sense of vitality, the divine within all of us. (Who can comprehend this mystery?) We can only see the shadow of its presence in the lives of others.

The social and spiritual revolutions of the twentieth century have released us from many clearly defined traditions and beliefs. Americans have responded to their release by a head long pursuit into materialism. Nearly all contemporary retirement planning begins and ends with financial planning. But that is not enough! What is man without a soul, a self? And how does he find happiness in the years after retirement, while he still has the power of choice! Now he has arrived at a time in his life time when he can say, "I will commit the years I have left in this world to something of lasting value."

Purpose Living each day with the desire to be useful, and in activities that enrich the lives of others.

Enthusiasm Connected to the Creator, who provides all the wisdom and energy that is ever needed to face the challenge of the moment.

Out of these three elements, MIND, BODY AND SPIRIT flow the yin and yang, masculine and feminine, together integrated: Giving rather than getting, influencing rather than demanding, accepting rather than asserting, living on for eternity in the light, knowing and being known.

FIXEN CAN BE FUN

THE EXPERTS SAY:

ANYONE CAN DO HOME MAINTENANCE IF
HE OR SHE HAS THE RIGHT TOOLS.

ADVICE FROM UNCLE BOB:

START WITH SIMPLE TASKS SUCH AS
SWATTING FLIES. IF YOU DO WELL,
CONSIDER BUYING A HACKSAW OR A
CRESCENT WRENCH.

AVOID PLUMBING AT ALL COSTS. NO LIFE
EXPERIENCE IS AS DEGRADING AS BEING
UNABLE TO SWEAT A JOINT!

IF YOU DON'T USE IT, YOU LOSE IT

I presented a speech at a service club recently, "SHIFTING GEARS TO NEW CAREERS IN THE LATER YEARS." I talked about the emotional adjustments to retirement that some experience. The sense of being rejected . . . the feelings of anger and frustration, the loss of self-esteem and the sadness that takes the edge off what other folks tell us is a great experience.

We talked about reentry and how to get involved in the many opportunities that are available. A recent survey by the American Association of Retired Persons (AARP) disclosed that retirees are being recruited by many businesses because retirees are reliable, have a strong work ethic, know how to get along with others, are seldom on street drugs, and have valuable work skills. Research indicates that most persons who retire at 60 to 65 return to some form of paid work or unpaid volunteering within two years.

Even the ancients shared this need for involvement. Seneca, the famous

Roman philosopher was recorded to have said, "I would rather be sick than idle." It makes me wonder if the work ethic had its roots in Rome rather than New England?

What are people choosing? The AARP survey indicates that retirees prefer jobs that involve being with other people, that provide for a sense of achievement, and that offer freedom of movement. Popular jobs include receptionists, tutors, grant writers, delivery persons, maintenance jobs, drivers, photographers, yard workers, and even fast-food restaurant clerks.

"Why bother to work?" a student asked me recently after a retirement planning class. I told him the observation I had heard from a prominent neurologist. He said, "When a patient has a back injury and chooses to drop out, there is a measurable decline in mental acuity, ability to express himself, and even the ability to maintain personal hygiene. This happens to people who are young: in their twenties and thirties."

The bottom line is "If you don't use it, you lose it."

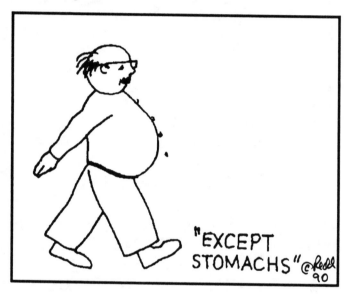

THE EXPERTS SAY:

THE BEST PLACE TO FIND TRANQUILITY IS
UNDER A TREE IN A QUIET WOODS.

ADVICE FROM UNCLE BOB:

AVOID WOODS THAT ARE INHABITED BY
BEARS, SKUNKS, OR CRAWLING INSECTS!

ALWAYS BRING A GROUND CLOTH, PORT-A-
JOHN, CAMP CHAIR, AND BATTERY- POWERED
TELEVISION. THERE IS NOTHING TO DO IN
THE WOODS EXCEPT SIT.

TRY TO FIND A TREE NEAR A PAVED ROAD SO
YOU DON'T HAVE TO WALK TOO FAR.

OUR MOST PRECIOUS HERITAGE

The fog hung low over the lake this morning as the sun glowed above the pines. "It's going to be a beautiful day," I shouted to Ann. She was curled in a ball under the covers, trying to enjoy just a few more winks. After all, it was Saturday!

Six-thirty might seem early for retirees to rise, but when the fish bite and the birds sing, I believe it is time to reawaken the neighborhood . . . starting with Ann.

As I watched the sky lighten, turning from a hazy pink-gray to rose and then a sparkling blue, it occurred to me that beyond all the turmoil described daily on TV and in the papers, there is the relentless reliability of nature. What a wonder to experience the absolute assurance that the sun will be there tomorrow morning when we pull up the bedroom blinds.

But all is not as it should be with man and nature. We read of the rain, forests being cut down, acid rain and oil spills . . . atrocity after atrocity. It has been this way for decades.

My Grandmother Zipf lived to be 102. At her one-hundredth birthday party, in 1965, I asked her, "What do you think of rockets in space and the planned trips to the moon?"

She quickly replied, "I think it is terrible. Everywhere people go they destroy things with commercialization. The next thing you know, they will put a Coca Cola sign on the moon and it will flash all night!"

She had seen so many changes: automobiles, airplanes, electricity, shopping centers—much "progress," and the price mankind had paid for it.

We seniors have a marvelous opportunity to become a part of actions to preserve our environment. What more important heritage can we pass to our children and grandchildren than the values that insist on restoration and preservation of our natural resources?

How can you help?

- Write your congressman. Every letter counts, and the number of votes is one number politicians take notice of.

- Volunteer to clean up your neighborhood.
- Support those organizations that fight for a clean environment: National Wildlife Federation, Sierra Club and others.

THE VICTORY GARDEN

THE EXPERTS SAY:

EVERY RETIREE SHOULD RAISE VEGETABLES IN AN ORGANIC GARDEN.

ADVICE FROM AUNT ANN:

BE CAREFUL NOT TO OVERFERTILIZE. IT'S VERY HARD TO HARVEST TOMATOES WHEN THEY ARE 20 FEET OFF THE GROUND!

START WITH RADISHES. IF THEY DON'T GROW NO ONE WILL NOTICE, AND YOU CAN DIG THEM UP AFTER DARK OR EASILY COVER THEM WITH "MULCH" ... WHATEVER THAT IS.

HOBBIES

Ann and I visited my cousin, Pauline, in Ohio last week and got an offer I could hardly refuse. She wanted to sell me 2500 plaster molds to make ceramic art objects. You know, like those plaques you hang on the wall.

Pauline is a hobby person. Hobbies are important, but for me they are like the "pursuit of excellence." I must never arrive, or the chase loses it's excitement. Pauline obviously had gone about as far as you can go with molded ceramic objects. She had glazed hundreds of items, given them to relatives, and sold them at flea markets. After that hobby, she pursued tole-painting, rug-hooking, and now she's into hand-painting T-shirts.

One of my hobbies is collecting antiques. I have spent a great portion of my life and energy collecting old furniture, refinishing it and passing the treasures off to my children.

Some folks plan their retirement around hobbies. They say, "When I retire, I'm finally going to have time to knit sweaters for my sister or build a birdhouse out of teak wood." I tell them to be careful. For some folks, hobbies are intriguing when they don't have time to spend on them. It may be that after retirement, making things might not be the most satisfying way to invest your time.

Hobbies can be an excellent source of supplementary income. But it's important to work out plans carefully. For instance, if you collect antiques, you might want to open an antique shop. Be sure to prepare a business plan and a realistic budget for it—or any business venture you decide to launch..

Skilled craftspersons can find many opportunities to market their hobby products, such as tole-painted objects, quilts or wooden puzzles at art fairs and in boutiques.

Or, if you are more interested in public affairs and public speaking, your interests could be expressed in a community political action activity or by writing a book. It's up to you. Truly, this is the land of the free and the home of the brave. We set our own limits.

"YOU LOOK GREAT"

I happened, by chance, to encounter an old friend downtown; she said,

"You look like you did 20 years ago."

Immediately several thoughts sprang into my mind: Is her eyesight failing? . . . has she forgotten who I am? . . . is she trying to be nice? In any case, I thanked her for her very kind compliment and proceeded down the street with an extra bounce in my step.

Is appearance a matter of age or attitude? Some folks over 60 say, "I have made my fortune," and they get downright sloppy about what they wear, how they shave, and even the frequency of baths. One classmate turned up at my fortieth high school reunion with a sport coat that looked like the one he had worn in 1947. Needless to say, he was noticed (and he had plenty of money to buy one without the belt in the back).

There is the matter of "overhang." I am not talking about the extension of a roof over the front porch. I am referring to that large appendage that extends forward from some men's bodies and stores enough reserves to keep them going without food for several winters. Other symptoms of the "who cares attitude" are frizzy hair, spotted ties, and dirty fingernails.

Let's face it, we seniors are the last generation that remembers what it meant to be smooth, sharp, classy, or if you are from Chicago, "Neato." We need to set an example for our children who pay $50 a pair for stone-bleached blue jeans or salty dog pants that even Charlie Chaplin would not have worn.

PRIDE–that's the word we need to proclaim to the younger generation. We can advocate standards of refinement–define for all to see what a lady or gentleman is–by the way we dress, the way we walk, the way we speak, the way we communicate with others.

"Who you are speaks so loudly, I can hardly hear what you are saying." Perhaps the young people would be less

susceptible to drugs, divorce, and poor
work habits if they had more **SELF
PRIDE.**

Is appearance important? You bet
it is. I have just ordered a light brown
hair piece from my barber. I suppose
some people will mistake me for my 30
year old son. That is the risk we take
when we grow young too quickly, but it
is worth the risk.

THE EXECUTIVE DREAM

THE EXPERTS SAY:

GOLFING EVERY DAY IS THE GREAT AMERICAN DREAM FOR MANY PRE-RETIREES.

ADVICE FROM UNCLE BOB:

A TEE IN THE ROUGH SAVES AT LEAST TWO STROKES!

PLAY FOR MONEY ONLY IF YOU KEEP SCORE AND YOUR OPPONENT GIVES YOU THREE "MULLIGANS."

PICK GOLF COURSES WITH SHORT FAIRWAYS, LARGE CUPS, NO HILLS, AND GOOD EATS, BECAUSE THE 19TH HOLE IS THE ONLY SURE JOY-GIVER.

WHO IS IN CHARGE AROUND HERE?

I just told my wife that I am not going to join another committee or volunteer for another "help me, Dad" program for the kids. In fact, it's gotten so bad that I may install green gravel in the backyard to avoid grass cutting and hide in the Upper Peninsula for the summer. She sat calmly sipping her tea and asked, "Now what's wrong?"

"Everything," I replied.

That was a slight exaggeration. But the essence of my problem is simple enough. Since retirement, I have discovered that the worse boss I ever had is now in charge. Being self-directed is a mixed blessing. It is harder to say **no** to myself than to a supervisor. And what gets to me most are the many temptations to get involved in just "one more" opportunity.

Let's take hobbies, for example. For years, refinishing antiques and gardening were sufficient. In the past year, I have added photography, TOASTMASTERS, a personal computer, and organ lessons to my list. Now that may not seem too bad, but then I took on teaching classes nights at a business college, helping at the Chamber of Commerce and writing a book.

Now, that still may not seem too bad, but then I signed up for the Elderhostel and made reservations for the national AARP convention and Senior Power Day. To this must be added visits with the grandchildren, maintaining the house (it needs painting), and cutting an acre of grass every ten days.

The bottom line is retirees are barraged with many tempting activities; the options are endless. So who decides how to use the time and energy we have, and what are the priorities? I have discovered that I must take responsibility for these choices. **I never had a tougher BOSS than I have now.**

RAPID ROBERT AND AUNT ANN
@ Redd 90

ANN SPEAKS OUT!

September 2, 1945, V. J. Day, September 5, 1954, our wedding day, July 1, 1986, Bob's retirement day are dates that are burned into my memory.

In 1986 after 32 years of marriage, the last 12 of which had been spent in relative freedom, Bob retired, came home and started applying his "management skills" to my domain. He was there for breakfast, all morning, lunch, all afternoon, dinner, all evening, and then all night in the king-sized bed.

His management advice was directed to sensitive areas, my appliances. I insisted that he **not** operate both the dishwasher and the washing machine at the same time. Never mix Clorox and ammonia, and use only one-quarter cup of soap powder.

His casual attitude toward details resulted in catastrophe when he put white clothing in with a new red shirt. Most of all, I objected to his standing behind me while I cooked and pulling out forgotten leftovers from the refrigerator with glee.

We have worked on these areas of conflict, and Bob has taken on new challenges beyond the home—thank goodness! He still pays too much attention to my activities, usually saying as I leave,

"Where are you going? And when will you be back?"

We have avoided some face-to-face conflicts by setting up a calendar and discussing the week ahead every Sunday night. But, I have to admit it is still not the same as it was before he retired. It never will be. That is what life is all about, adjusting to change. Now I spend most of my idle moments, the few I have, answering the phone for "him" or hiding in the bathroom reading a novel (Bob does not think I should read fiction and tells me so whenever he catches me).

The key to it all is keeping a sense of humor. There are many positives. We can take trips whenever we want, and there is much more flexibilty for visiting children and grandchildren.

There is life for the wife after the retirement of her spouse, but it requires patience, planning, foresight, and above all good communications. **These are really the best years of our lives.**

THE SPIRITUAL CONNECTION

THE EXPERTS SAY:

ATTENDING A CHURCH OR A SYNAGOGUE
IS IMPORTANT TO KEEP US ON THE RIGHT
TRACK.

ADVICE FROM UNCLE BOB:

A STRONG RELIGIOUS CONNECTION IS
ESSENTIAL AS WE FACE THE ADVERSITIES
OF AGING. FAITH IN GOD IS A CONSTANT
SOURCE OF STRENGTH AND GUIDANCE.

THIS IS A MATTER THAT SHOULD RECEIVE
SPECIAL ATTENTION BY THOSE FEW
RETIREES WHO ARE HABITUAL SINNERS!

IN CONCLUSION...

After observing many friends, relatives, and acquaintances who are experiencing the wonderful years after 50, we have concluded that each person or couple finds a unique way to adjust to the changes aging invokes.

Within the limits placed upon them by their health, they search out ways to satisfy their needs and aspirations; first for food and shelter, then beyond that for recognition, creativity, and a sense of purpose. Whether it is in building a legacy of love with their children and grandchildren or building a new home each found happiness through a sense of purpose that filled their days..

Often the selection of activities is an expression of gentle competition . . . playing golf, tennis, shuffle board or indoor sports like bridge, gin-rummy or checkers. Others pursue the arts, painting, needle-crafts, or rock polishing, while others express themselves through social action activities such as politics, literacy training or hospice.

Unfortunately, some folks are inhibited by past experiences and retreat as they grow older. They seek "happiness" by attaching themselves to a subservient spouse or their children.

These are the choices of the "prime time" years. For some they will be years filled with joy–for others, loneliness and frustration.

We hope these writings have provided you with hints that will help you plan for the years after 50 or enhance your present life-style if you are already past that landmark age.

Relax as you enjoy the flowing river of the years. Sometimes they will be easy drifting days; sometimes terrifying rapids of adversity. But we have always found that the crisis passes, the answers come, and the healing powers of the life force within us is amazing.

As you face the challenges of life, remember that you will never be defeated by adversity, but you may be setback if you lose perspective and focus on your losses rather than on the positive possibilities each day offers.

A sense of humor is your most important resource. It is the most valuable gift given to us by our Creator, and the highest form of wisdom.

We both hope you will always keep your fountain of good humor flowing with warm sparkles of love for all you meet.

Ann and Robert Redd

INDEX OF ARTICLES AND CARTOONS

(A)   Articles
(C) Cartoons

	Page No
Chapter 1	**13**

* **Money Grows on Trees(C)** — 15
* **Smooth Transitions (A)** — 16
* **What's Important (A)** — 18-19
* **The Last Day (C)** — 20
* **Going to Bees (A)** — 21-22
* **Nutrition or Attrition (C)** — 23
* **More So (A)** — 24-25
* **There is Good News and Bad News (C)** — 26
* **What You Will Be is What You Are! (A)** — 27-30

Chapter 2 — **31**

* **Where is My Lunch (C)** — 33
* **But Not For Lunch (A)** — 34-36
* **Is There Romance After 50 (A)** — 37-39
* **Wife Time Secrets (A)** — 40-41
* **When Will You Be Back (A)** — 42-44
* **Dancing (C)** — 45
* **Fun and Games We Play (A)** — 46-48
* **Matters of the Heart (A)** — 49-50
* **Granpa's Little Buddy (C)** — 51
* **Grand-Parenting (A)** — 52-53
* **Never Drop a Neighbors Piano (C)** — 54

INDEX ARTICLE AND CARTOONS

Chapter 2 (Continued)	Page No
• For the Best of Futures (A)	55-56
• Buried Treasures (C)	57
• Possessed By Possessions (A)	58-60
• Man's Best Friend (C)	61
• We Have Gone to the Dogs(A)	62-64
• Vacations Redefined (A)	65-66
• So What's New About Recycling (A)	67-69

Chapter 3	71
• Better Safe than Sorry (C)	72
• Snowbirds (A)	73-75
• Escape to Paradise (A)	76-78
• Moving Day (C)	79
• To Move or Not to Move (A)	80-81
• Moving to Arizona (A)	82-83
• The Big Trip (C)	84

Chapter 4	85
• The Healthy Hike (C)	87
• The Secret of a Long Joyful Life (A)	88-91
• Fixin Can Be Fun (C)	92
• If You Don't Use It You Lose It (A)	93-95

INDEX OF ARTICLES AND CARTOONS
(A) Articles
(C) Cartoons

Chapter 4 (Continued)   Page No

* **Peace and Quiet (C))**   96
* **Our Precious Heritage (A)**   97-99
* **Victory Garden (C)**   100
* **Hobbies (A)**   101-102
* **You Look Great (A)**   103-105
* **The Executive Dream (C)**   106
* **Who is in Charge? (A)**   107-108
* **Ann Speaks Out (A)**   109-110
* **The Spiritual Connection (C)**   111
* **In Conclusion (A)**   112-114

* **Index**   115-117
* **About the Authors**   118-119
* **Order Forms**
* **Request for Comments**

ABOUT THE AUTHORS

Bob retired from a 20 year career in public accounting and redirected his life into a new career of teaching retirement planning. Ann, his wife joined him in this venture, and together they have presented classes for the employees of numerous corporations including: Amway Corporation, AT&T, Foremost Insurance Company, Mazda Distributors Great Lakes, and others.

In 1989, Bob's book *Achievers Never Quit* was published. It discusses the emotional impact of retirement on the family and the activity options open to retirees in the 1990's. It has had excellent acceptance and is being used by many companies in their retirement planning classes.

Ann and Bob combined their skills to produce *Whimsey, Wit, and Wisdom* which they hope will be enjoyable and helpful to folks over 50, whether they are still working or have retired.

They have been married 36 years, have 3 adult children, 7 grandchildren and a large black Doberman named "Hedwig."

Both are college graduates with many interests and hobbies. Ann teaches traditional rug hooking and is the past-president of a national rug hooking association.

The Thornapple Publishing Company
P.O. Box 256
Ada, Michigan 49301
616-676-1583

YES! Please enter my order for ____ copies of
WHIMSEY, WIT AND WISDOM (ISBN 1-877756-03-2)

☐ Check   ☐ Money Order   ☐ Purchase Order No._____
☐ MasterCard

Credit Card No. ☐☐☐☐ ☐☐☐☐ ☐☐☐☐ ☐☐☐☐

Expiration Date ☐☐ ☐☐   _____
⠀⠀⠀⠀⠀⠀⠀⠀⠀⠀Month⠀Year⠀Signature

If I am not completely satisfied, I may return the book(s)
within 60 days for a full refund or credit.

_____Copies of WHIMSEY, WIT AND WISDOM @ $8.95 _____

Shipping and handling @ $2.00 per copy _____

Michigan residents please add 6% sales tax _____

Total _____

Mail to:

The Thornapple Publishing Company
P.O. Box 256
Ada, Michigan 49301

REQUEST FOR COMMENTS

We would be very interested to learn about your retirement experiences or comments about this book. To communicate with Ann or Bob Redd, just write us a note at the address shown below.

Ann or Bob Redd
P.O.Box 56
Ada, Michigan, 49301